VOCAL SELECTIONS FROM COLE PORTER'S
KISS ME, KATE

T0053195

"IT'S SURE-FIRE!" —WALTER WINCHELL

SAINT SUBBER & LEMUEL AYERS
present

ALFRED   PATRICIA
DRAKE · MORISON IN

KISS
ME,
KATE

with
HAROLD   LISA
LANG · KIRK

choreography by HANYA HOLM
musical director PEMBROKE DAVENPORT
orchestrations by ROBERT RUSSELL BENNETT

music and lyrics by
COLE PORTER
book by SAM and BELLA SPEWACK
settings and costumes by LEMUEL AYERS
production staged by JOHN C. WILSON

CENTURY THEATRE
7th AVENUE and 59th STREET
MATINEES WEDNESDAY and SATURDAY

Produced by
Alfred Music Publishing Co., Inc.
P.O. Box 10003
Van Nuys, CA 91410-0003
alfred.com

Printed in USA.

ISBN-10: 0-7390-7312-5
ISBN-13: 978-0-7390-7312-4

Cover image from *Hallmark Hall of Fame's* presentation of *Kiss Me, Kate*, broadcast on NBC on November 20, 1958. Shown, from left to right: Alfred Drake, Patricia Morison, and Julie Wilson (Photofest/National Broadcasting Company). Baroque ornament: © iStockphoto / Scott Krycia

Unless otherwise indicated, photos and images are courtesy of the Cole Porter Music and Literary Property Trusts; Peter Felcher, Trustee, and Roberta Staats, Executive Director. Additional thanks to Robert Kimball and Patricia Morison.

 Alfred Cares. Contents printed on 100% recycled paper, except pages 1–4 which are printed on 60% recycled paper.

Anne Jeffreys (Lilli/Kate) slams her tankard for emphasis in a performance of "I Hate Men." Jeffreys replaced Patricia Morison in the original Broadway production of *Kiss Me, Kate* (Photofest).

The two gangsters (Jack Diamond and Harry Clark) sing the uproarious "Brush Up Your Shakespeare," from the original Broadway production of *Kiss Me, Kate* (Photofest).

Brian Stokes Mitchell (Fred/Petruchio) in the 1999 Broadway revival (Joan Marcus/Photofest).

CONTENTS

45 rpm box set of the original Broadway cast recording (Collection of Cary Ginell).

The famous spanking scene from *Kiss Me, Kate*, featuring Alfred Drake and Patricia Morison (Photofest).

French poster for the 1953 film version. (Photofest).

Scene from the 1953 film version of *Kiss Me Kate*. Standing behind the donkey are stars Howard Keel (Fred/Petruchio) and Kathryn Grayson (Lilli/Kate) (MGM/Photofest).

Brian Stokes Mitchell (Fred/Petruchio) and Marin Mazzie (Lilli/Kate) in the 1999 Broadway revival of *Kiss Me, Kate* (Joan Marcus/Photofest © Joan Marcus).

Brent Barrett (Fred/Petruchio) and Rachel York (Lilli/Kate) starred in the 2003 television production, broadcast on PBS (PBS/Photofest © PBS).

Cole Porter, during the original Broadway production of *Kiss Me, Kate*.

Introduction
BRUSHING UP SHAKESPEARE

The musical production *Kiss Me, Kate* could not have come at a more opportune time in the life and career of Cole Porter. In the spring of 1948, Porter, who was used to having hit after hit, had experienced three flops in a row: the Broadway musicals *Seven Lively Arts* and *Around the World in Eighty Days* (the latter produced by Orson Welles) and the MGM film *The Pirate* (starring box-office sensations Judy Garland and Gene Kelly). The prevailing notion amongst the press and the public was that Porter's best days were behind him, and at the age of 57, he began to believe that his stature as one of show business' most prolific and successful composers had become irrevocably tarnished. Faced with an increasingly bleak future, he was actually considering writing a score for a show by a soap opera writer when his attention was directed to a proposed musical version of William Shakespeare's comedy *The Taming of the Shrew.*

Cole Porter and *Kiss Me, Kate*
author Bella Spewack confer
during a rehearsal.

The idea to transform *The Taming of the Shrew* into a musical originated with Arnold Saint Subber, a young stage manager, and Lemuel Ayers, a designer of sets and costumes. Saint Subber had witnessed a backstage quarrel between Alfred Lunt and Lynn Fontanne during a performance of *Shrew* and thought the argument would make a great sketch. Subber and Ayers talked playwright Bella Spewack into writing the book for a proposed musical and the three began discussing possible storylines. Spewack eventually recruited her husband and writing partner Samuel into completing the book. Spewack was never fond of Shakespeare's original but thought it could work on Broadway if it were given a different context, so she decided to turn it into a behind-the-scenes look at the staging of a Broadway-bound production of *Shrew,* starring an embattled ex-husband-and-wife. When it came time to select someone to write the score, Saint Subber and Ayers first chose Burton Lane, whose *Finian's Rainbow* was then the toast of Broadway. When Lane proved to be unavailable, Spewack suggested Porter. The producers, claiming that Porter was on his way out as a Broadway force, could not talk Spewack out of it and reluctantly went along with her choice.

When approached by Spewack, Porter was initially repelled by the idea, believing that the concept was too highbrow and would not have sufficient mass appeal, ignoring the fact that his own songs had thrived in such a fashion for years. Spewack, however, was not to be rebuffed, and after much brow-beating and wheedling, she wore Porter down until he consented to write the score. *Kiss Me, Kate* was not only a smash hit of the 1948–49 season, it became the most successful and best-loved musical of Porter's career. His score was rife with rip-roaring humor, outrageous contemporary references, and touching sentimentality as he utilized all of his musical experience in creating songs drawn from jazz, vaudeville, and even old Vienna. It would become one of the most admired and honored scores in Broadway history. The original Broadway production, which starred Alfred Drake and Patricia Morison, ran for over 1,000 performances and, in 1949, won five Tony Awards®, including Best Musical and Best Composer and Lyricist. A film version, shot in 3-D starring Howard Keel and Kathryn Grayson, was released in 1953. Drake and Morison returned in 1958 to star in a television production for *Hallmark Hall of Fame,* with Julie Wilson playing the role filled by Lisa Kirk in the original Broadway cast. *Kiss Me, Kate* was popularly revived in 1999 in a production starring Brian Stokes Mitchell and Marin Mazzie. This version won five Tony Awards including Best Revival of a Musical.

THE SONGS OF KISS ME, KATE

Act I

Kiss Me, Kate opens with "Another Op'nin', Another Show," a jubilant, high-kicking ensemble number that has since become a show-biz anthem, often used outside the context of the musical. In the original cast, the number was led by Annabelle Hill as Hattie, costumer for temperamental movie star Lilli Vanessi (played by Patricia Morison).

Lilli and her ex-husband Fred Graham (Alfred Drake) are starring as Katherine and Petruchio, respectively, in a Baltimore production of a musical version of *The Taming of the Shrew*. Lois Lane (played by Lisa Kirk) and her boyfriend Bill Calhoun (Harold Lang) are also featured in the Shakespeare play, portraying Bianca and Lucentio. In "Why Can't You Behave?," Lois chides Bill for his incessant gambling. Bill has used Fred's name on his I.O.U. to two thugs (played by Jack Diamond and Harry Clark) who come to issue Fred an ultimatum to pay up or else.

During a break, Fred and Lilli reminisce about a more romantic time in their lives when they co-starred in an operetta together. In the song "Wunderbar," Porter spoofs the world of Viennese operetta (which he helped usurp in the 1920s), deftly walking the line between schmaltz and unabashed sentimentality. When Lilli receives flowers from Fred, which were mistakenly sent to her instead of to Lois, she realizes she still loves Fred and sings "So in Love." The song's heartfelt lyrics have none of the cynicism that became a hallmark of many of Porter's most celebrated songs. "So in Love" not only became the hit ballad of the show, but also a pop standard, with successful versions recorded by Dinah Shore, Patti Page, and Gordon MacRae, among others.

As the show-within-the-show begins, the four principals (Petruchio, Katherine, Lucentio, and Bianca) sing the inviting "We Open in Venice" as they stroll along the streets of Padua. It is then revealed that Lucentio (Bill) may not marry Bianca (Lois) until her older sister Katherine (Lilli) is wed first. (It is this custom, which is common in Jewish tradition, that helped Spewack convince Porter to write the score for *Kiss Me, Kate*. Porter was always enamored of using Jewish-sounding elements in his songs and believed they were keys to the success of hits such as "Love for Sale" and "My Heart Belongs to Daddy.") As the play progresses, Bianca revels in recalling her many suitors in the flippant "Tom, Dick or Harry."

Petruchio (Fred) enters the scene and sings "I've Come to Wive It Wealthily in Padua," with the first two lines taken directly from Shakespeare's play; the male chorus repeats his lines much like in a Gilbert and Sullivan operetta. In this song, Porter mixes Shakespearean words and phrases with contemporary references as he declares he is on the hunt for "a damsel I'll make my dame." Kate responds with the declaration "I Hate Men," in which she rebuffs Petruchio's advances with ill-tempered abandon. To punctuate her character's role, Patricia Morison employed a prop—a tray loaded with metal pie plates—that she would summarily slam with a beer tankard, scattering dishes every which way with a loud clatter that jolted

Lilli Vanessi (Patricia Morison) sings "So in Love" from the original Broadway production of *Kiss Me, Kate* (Photofest).

audiences; sometimes the flying dishes even found their way into the orchestra pit. At *Kiss Me, Kate*'s opening in Philadelphia, the number stopped the show.

When Lilli discovers that the flowers she received from Fred were meant for Lois, she becomes furious. Fred attempts to woo her back when he (as Petruchio) sings "Were Thine That Special Face" to her. Lilli threatens to resign from the company regardless, so Fred tells the two gangsters that if they can keep her from leaving, he will pay them the money they are owed. They agree and take on roles in *Shrew* so that they can keep their eyes on Lilli.

The ensemble song "I Sing of Love," led by Lois and Bill, is sung toward the end of Act I. Written in the form of a tarantella, it includes two patter sections that show Porter at his most playful as he rhymes "rivers" and "cold shivers" with the line "My nerves grown tense / When radios commence / Commercial songs to flush livers."

Act II

In the second act opener, the cast of *The Taming of the Shrew* is taking a break in the alley in back of the theater, trying to cool off from the stifling summer heat. Although the lyrics to the ensuing number, "Too Darn Hot," claim that the weather prevents the characters from engaging in strenuous amorous activities, this apparently does not apply to the steamy dancing that goes on during the song. The racy lyrics resulted in "Too Darn Hot" being banned from radio airplay in middle America.

Fred Graham/Petruchio (Alfred Drake) and Lilly Vanessi/Kate (Patricia Morison) act out a scene from *The Taming of the Shrew* in *Kiss Me, Kate* (Photofest).

Back on the set, Petruchio (Fred) and Katherine (Lilli) have just been married, but when Katherine locks him out of their bedroom, Petruchio shows he is already regretting his decision as he sings the soliloquy "Where Is the Life That Late I Led?" The title comes directly from Shakespeare, but the lyrics constitute one of Porter's most hilarious catalog songs, as Petruchio recalls previous female conquests in classic mock-Italian opera form.

In their dressing room, the fickle Lois explains to Bill that her many love affairs have had no effect on her feelings toward him. The title "Always True to You in My Fashion" comes from Victorian poet Ernest Dowson's "Cynara!" but Porter embellished Dowson's theme with a litany of Lois's past paramours, ranging from oil tycoons to Clark Gable. Bill, in turn, sings of his love for her, pledging to "give up coffee for Sanka," rhyming it with Bianca. (Porter even inserts his own name into the second verse, which was written for the published version of the song.)

"Brush Up Your Shakespeare" is the show-stopping "11 o'clock number" of *Kiss Me, Kate*. Sung by the two boorish gangsters who are trying to collect their money from Fred, the song is not really essential to the plot, but is a showcase for Porter's masterful combining of Shakespearean references with the characters' Damon Runyon street slang and malaprops. The two hoods have discovered that their gangster boss, who is owed money, has been summarily rubbed out, thus making the debt unnecessary. Since this makes the characters similarly superfluous, there remained the need for them to be somehow shunted off stage. It was the idea of one of Porter's friends, agent Robert Raison, that the two toughs be allowed to sing themselves into the wings.

Their duet on "Brush Up Your Shakespeare" became a zany, goofy masterpiece. In the song, Porter forces words to rhyme as if he were holding a gun to their heads, among them, changing "ambassador" to "embissida" so that it would rhyme with "Troilus and Cressida."

"From This Moment On," written in 1950, was to be included in Porter's lampoon of Greek mythology *Out of This World*, but was dropped before the show's Broadway opening. In 1953, it was inserted into the movie *Kiss Me Kate*, where it became a dance showcase for Bob Fosse and Ann Miller. Its appearance in the film version resulted in the song becoming one of Porter's most popular numbers. It was reinserted into the stage version for the 1999 revival.

In the final scene, as Lilli ultimately decides to return to Fred, she uses the words of Shakespeare to express her feelings towards him. "I Am Ashamed That Women Are So Simple" is sung in character, and Porter retains nearly all of the Bard's words, with only slight alterations.

In this songbook, we have included two numbers that were never used in the original production of *Kiss Me, Kate*, although they were eventually recorded. The release for "We Shall Never Be Younger," was later used in "No Lover" from *Out of This World*. The song was cut from *Kiss Me, Kate* because its somber message, sung by Patricia Morison in previews, reduced audiences to tears. "What Does Your Servant Dream About" is an ensemble number that was slated for Act II, but was also relegated to the stack of songs that didn't make the cut.

On the set of the 1953 film version of *Kiss Me Kate*. Seated, left to right: Cole Porter, Kathryn Grayson (Lilli), Ann Miller (Lois). Standing: director George Sidney, Howard Keel (Fred), producer Jack Cummings.

During the time *Kiss Me, Kate* was being produced, Cole Porter was suffering from a variety of physical maladies, including an ulcer and persistent shin pain from a collision with his Schipperke dog. Through all this discomfort, as well as the depression he was experiencing due to his run of professional misfortunes, it was a wonder that Porter wrote such brilliantly romantic songs as "So in Love" and expansive, hilarious numbers like "Brush Up Your Shakespeare." Even up to the night of the opening, when his friends told him that *Kiss Me, Kate* would be the biggest smash of his career, Porter dreaded yet another flop. His fears, however, were unwarranted. After the Broadway premiere, Porter attended a cast party held at a lavish apartment of one of the show's backers. As Porter entered the foyer, Saint Subber, who was standing on a second floor landing, waved a copy of the *New York Times* and yelled down at him, "Cole! The *Times* is out and it's a hit!" Porter, who rarely walked without the aid of a cane because of a debilitating horseback riding accident sustained in 1937, threw his cane to the floor and bounded up the grand marble staircase, unassisted, to greet Saint Subber. It was probably the proudest moment of his life.

Cary Ginell
Popular Music Editor
Alfred Music Publishing Co., Inc.

THE ORIGINAL KATE REMEMBERS

I came to Hollywood in 1938 after I finished doing *The Two Bouquets*, an operetta that Marc Connelly directed. Alfred Drake was my leading man, and while we were doing that show, I was testing for film and Alfred and I used to go out late at night and talk. We couldn't afford Sardi's so we used to sit up all night at a Childs restaurant and talk theater, and I remember Alfred saying to me, "Don't go out there. They'll never know what to do with you." But when I finished the show, Paramount picked me up and I went to Hollywood.

Ten years later, when I was hired for *Kate*, I had just finished *Song of the Thin Man*, which was the last Thin Man movie that William Powell and Myrna Loy did. I was the bad girl in that movie. I was seriously studying voice and my manager told me that Cole Porter had a house on Rockingham Avenue and he took me out to sing for him. It wasn't for anything in particular; it was just so I could get used to singing again. So I went to his house and I purposely sang Rodgers and Hammerstein. When I finished, he handed me the script for *Kiss Me, Kate*. At that time, he was having trouble raising money for it. Finally, on a Saturday, I got a call that it was going to be done and the producers wanted me to sing for them. The next Monday, I was supposed to start working on a television series called *The Cases of Eddie Drake*, but my agent told me to fly to New York to audition for *Kate*. The people in New York had an opera star in mind but Cole wanted me. They thought he was crazy and told him, "She's not a singer, she's a movie star." I had not been known as a singer, but I had studied very hard for quite a few years but nobody knew that I had this voice. So I sang for these skeptical producers and all of a sudden they were all over me. Cole called me when I got back, told me that they all liked me, and I got the part. Television was new at that time and *Eddie Drake* was being produced by a little independent company. I played a woman psychiatrist to whom the detective told his stories. All my scenes were in the office so they said, "We'll shoot all your scenes in one week, but we want you to promise to publicize the show when you get to Broadway." And that's how I got to New York.

Cole was a very, very dear friend and he was very helpful to me. For some reason or other, I think he liked me, so I didn't let him down. He used to come to rehearsals nearly every day, elegantly dressed with a flower in his buttonhole. And he'd sit in a chair in the middle aisle and listen. He had a thing about hearing a lyric. We didn't have microphones then and you weren't supposed to shout or scream, you were supposed to use your voice properly, but if he couldn't hear something, he'd toot a little whistle that he carried around and say, "I didn't hear that last lyric." As sophisticated as Cole Porter was, his songs were easy to sing because he was such a terrific artist.

We rehearsed at the New Amsterdam Theatre. If something new was needed during rehearsals, Cole would climb up to the old piano on the stage in his elegant suit with his bad leg and he'd write something else for us, right then and there. He wrote one lyric for "I Hate Men" that we never used. I still have it on his letterhead from when we were in Philadelphia:

> Avoid my dear the British peer who gives thine ear a jawful,
> You'll settle down in London town and live in wedlock lawful.
> Your relations may be pleasant, quite, but his are always awful.

When I was in drama school at the Neighborhood Playhouse, I took dance with Martha Graham. I never danced professionally, but I would use it in my performance. When I was rehearsing "I Hate Men," everyone who heard those lyrics told me, "When you sing that song, it's going to make you look terrible." So I went to Cole and told him that everyone in the cast thought that I shouldn't be singing this song. He said, "Patricia, I remember a Victor Herbert operetta called *Mlle. Modiste* where there was a guy sitting at a table with a tankard in his hand, singing 'I want what I want when I want it' and then, bang!" And he said, "You just hit that tankard on something and don't worry." A lot of the movements that I did I figured out by myself. My Martha Graham training helped me move around the table. When I sang "So in Love," there was an interval in the score where the orchestra is playing, and it says in the score, "Lilli moves about the stage." Well, I'm holding the wedding bouquet that Fred had sent to Lois Lane, but mistakenly it came to me. So during the interval, I get up and go to my dressing table, and I take the bouquet and kiss it and put it down. I worked that out also. Of course, in the next Shakespeare scene, I throw it at him.

A lot of the battles Alfred and I had on the set we worked out. There was a scene where there was a table between us and I had to lean against that table so hard that I eventually got bruises on my thighs. In another scene I have to slap his face. Well, I always learned to slap him on the side of the neck with a cupped hand, but one night I missed and I hit him right on the button and down he went. In another scene, my hair is down and Petruchio says, "How, now, Kate?", slaps me on my back, and my hair falls over my face. So I push it back and he does it again. The next time he does it, I leave it there, so he separates it and I stick my tongue out at him and he pushes me into the bedroom. On matinee days, we could hear the ladies in the audience saying, "That's not her real hair; that's a wig." So Alfred started yanking my hair just to show them it was really mine.

Patricia Morison, early 1950s (Photofest).

When we had to cut a song, Cole didn't hesitate. There was a wonderful song in the first act called "We Shall Never Be Younger." I remember the day they cut it. I think it was kind of silly to cut it because it's such a beautiful song. "We shall never be younger than we are today." It's a lovely, lovely song and I'm glad it's included in this songbook.

Sam and Bella Spewack were wonderful, interesting people. Sam wasn't involved much at the beginning, but when they were working on "Brush Up Your Shakespeare," that's when Sam got into it and eventually got co-billing as a writer with Bella. Bella was a very fiery, colorful lady. She was very directly honest. I remember when someone in the male chorus told her how much he admired her, she said, "Oh, stop being so servile!"

When it came time for opening night in Philadelphia, we had no idea how the show would do. We hadn't even heard Robert Russell Bennett's orchestrations yet. That day, we heard the orchestrations for the first time and all of a sudden, we thought, "Oh, my God." On opening night, the audience went crazy. That first night was something amazing. From that night on, there were lines all around the block. We were thrilled and astonished. I remember Cole came with his wife Linda and his mother. Afterward, he came backstage and said, "My mother thought you were wonderful." And I said to him, "Do you mean she wouldn't come backstage to see me?" The next night, this darling little replica of Cole Porter came to my dressing room and said, "Cole said I should come backstage." And do you know her name was Kate, too?

I really enjoyed playing Lilli, on Broadway, in summer stock, and for a year in London. When you sing the songs in this book, bring your own personality to the part. You don't have to do anything the way I did; you can find your own character. As Polonius says in *Hamlet*, "To thine own self be true."

Patricia Morison
July 14, 2010

ANOTHER OP'NIN', ANOTHER SHOW

Words and Music by
COLE PORTER

Very lively (♩ = 152)

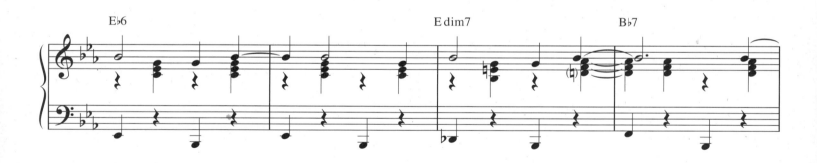

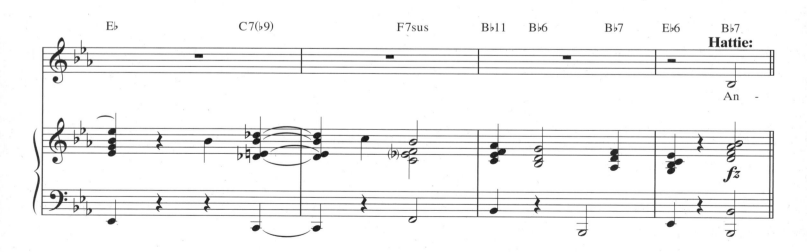

Another Op'nin', Another Show - 8 - 1

16

Lois Lane (Lisa Kirk) sings "Why Can't You Behave?" to her gambling boyfriend Bill Calhoun (Harold Lang) in the original Broadway production of *Kiss Me, Kate* (Photofest).

WHY CAN'T YOU BEHAVE?

Words and Music by
COLE PORTER

Why can't you be - have?_____ Oh, why can't you be -

have?_____ Af - ter all the things you told me and the

Why Can't You Behave? - 5 - 1

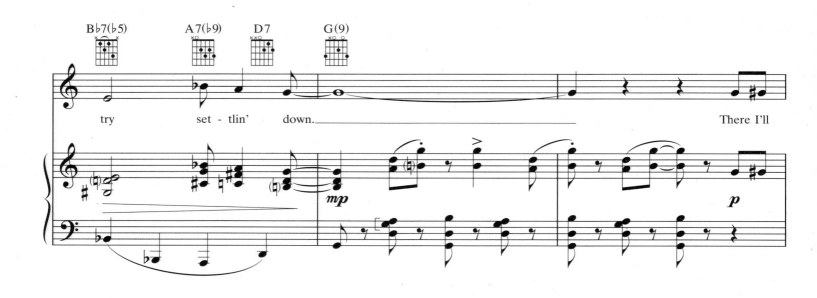

*In subsequent editions the bracketed lyric has been replaced with, "'cause you're all in the world I crave."

WUNDERBAR

Words and Music by
COLE PORTER

Lyrics:
Gaz-ing down on the Jung-frau from our se-cret cha-let for two,____ let us drink, Lieb-chen mein, in the moon-light be-nign, to the joy of our

bar!_____ Wun - der - bar,_____ wun - der - bar!_____

C/D   G

___ We're a - lone and hand in glove,_____ not a

D7

cloud near or far,_____ why it's

G

more than wun - der - bar!_____ Oh, I

SO IN LOVE

Words and Music by
COLE PORTER

So in Love - 6 - 1

Steady moderate tempo, not slowly

Refrain:

taunt me_____ and hurt me,_____ de-
ceive me,_____ de - sert me._____ I'm
yours 'til I die,_____ so in
love,_____ so in love,_____ so in

cresc.

f *passionately*

WE OPEN IN VENICE

Words and Music by
COLE PORTER

TOM, DICK OR HARRY

Words and Music by
COLE PORTER

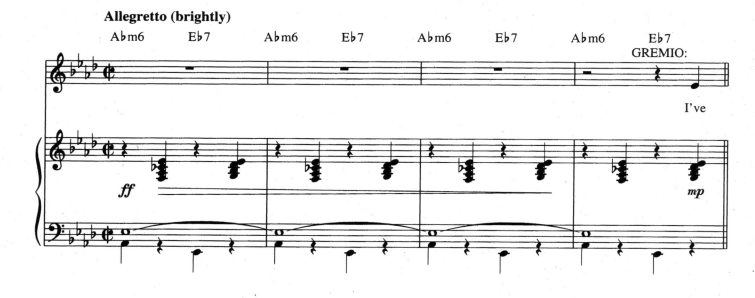

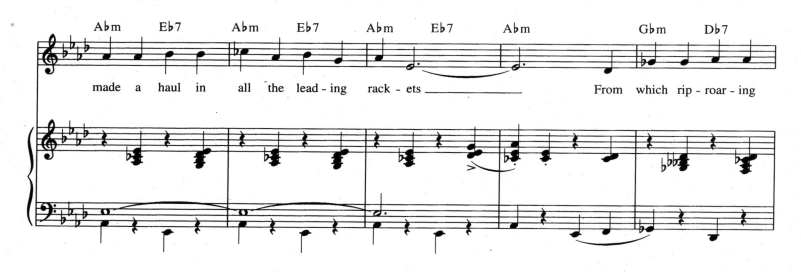

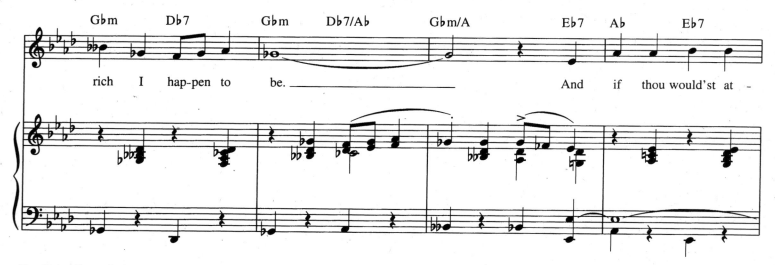

Tom, Dick or Harry - 8 - 1

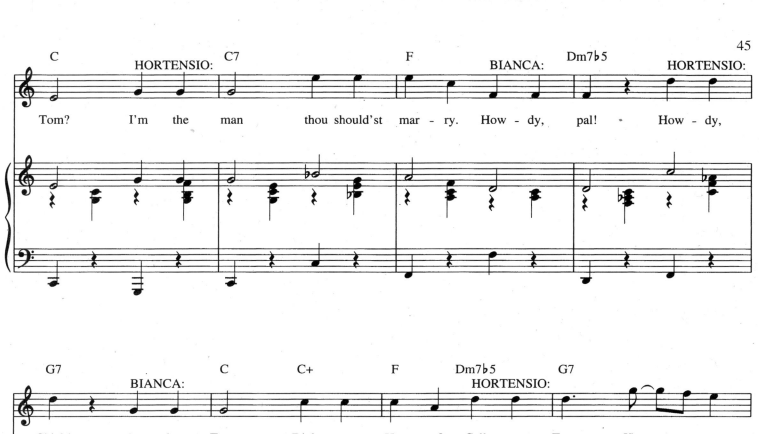

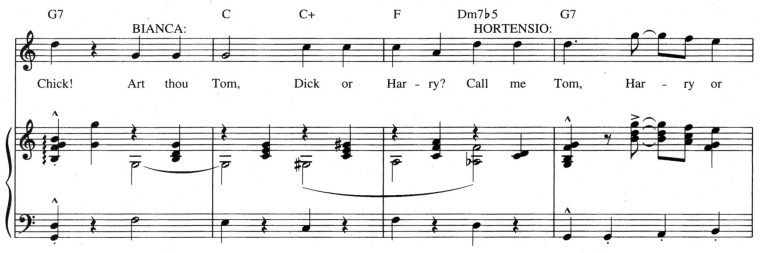

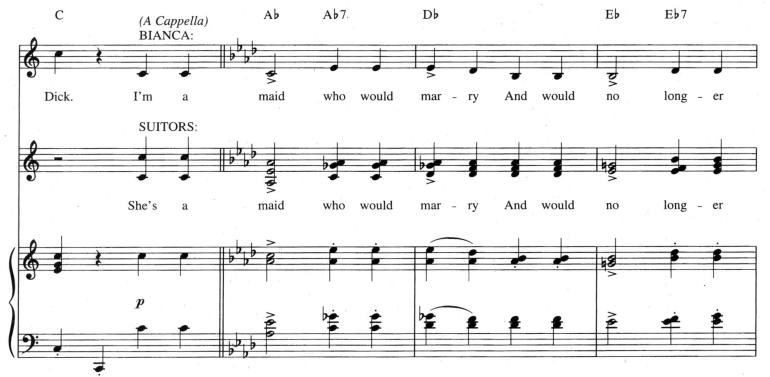

Tom, Dick or Harry - 8 - 6

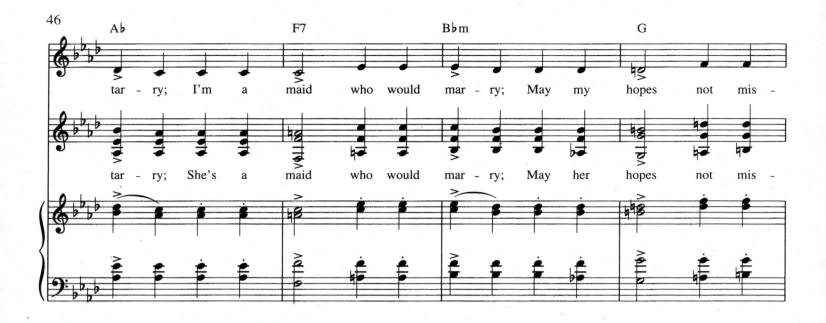

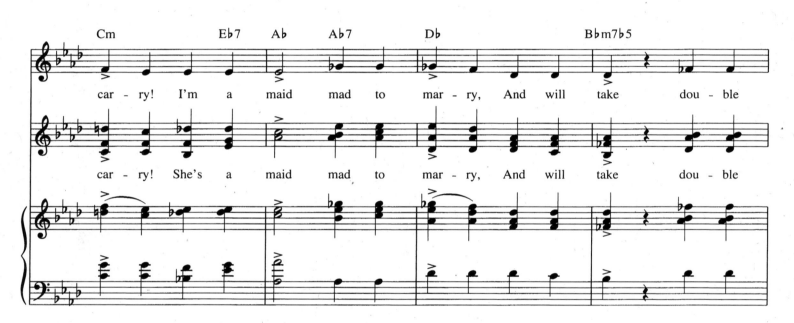

I'VE COME TO WIVE IT WEALTHILY
IN PADUA

Words and Music by
COLE PORTER

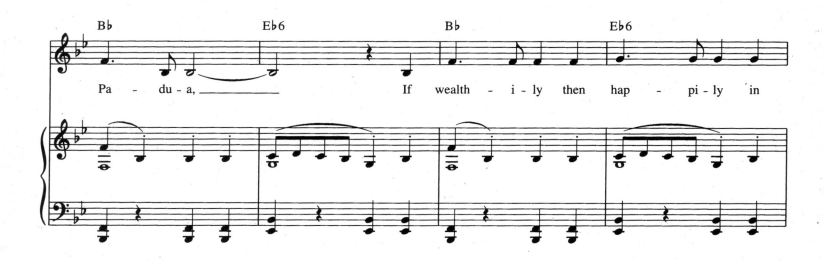

I've Come to Wive It Wealthily in Padua - 7 - 1

I HATE MEN

Words and Music by
COLE PORTER

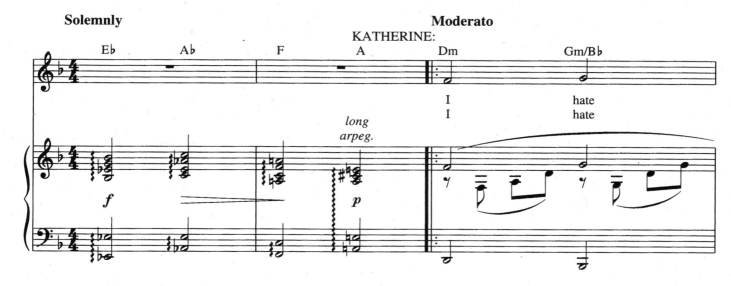

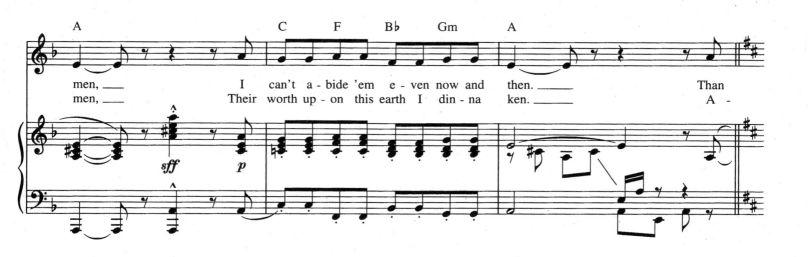

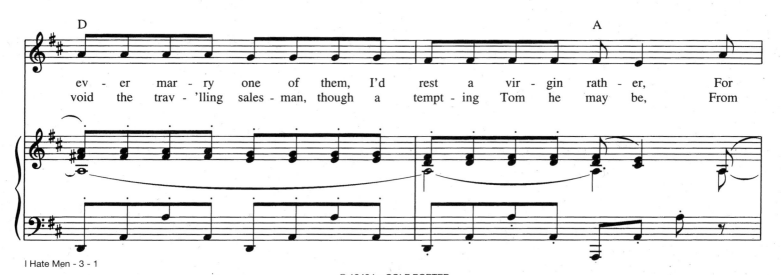

I Hate Men - 3 - 1

WERE THINE THAT SPECIAL FACE

Words and Music by
COLE PORTER

Andantino con moto

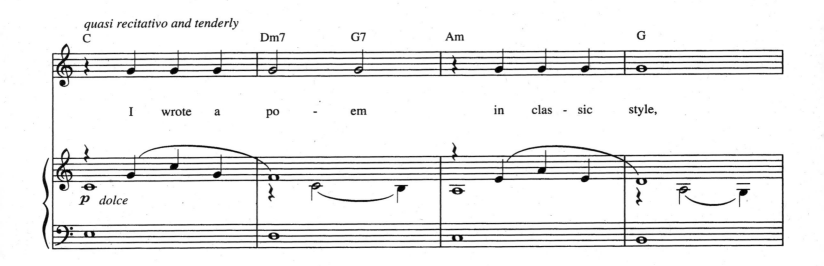

quasi recitativo and tenderly

I wrote a po - em in clas - sic style,

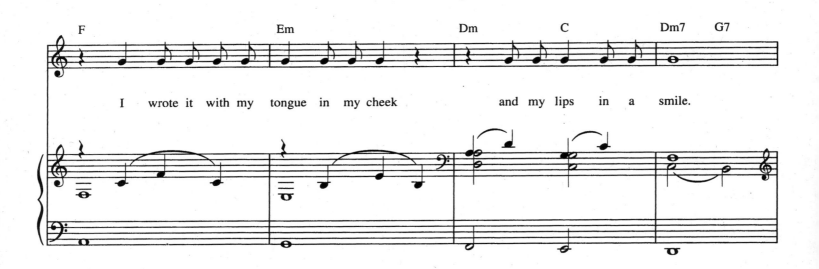

I wrote it with my tongue in my cheek and my lips in a smile.

Were Thine That Special Face - 4 - 1

I SING OF LOVE

Words and Music by
COLE PORTER

Optional Patter 2 lyrics (for Encore):
I loathe all the songs about rivers,
From spring songs I get the cold shivers.
My nerves grow tense
When radios commence
Commercial songs to flush livers.
My hands always get a bit clammy
When Jolson revives his ole mammy.
Of what do I sing if you request it?
This time, you guessed it.

TOO DARN HOT

Words and Music by
COLE PORTER

Too Darn Hot - 8 - 8

WHERE IS THE LIFE THAT LATE I LED?

Words and Music by
COLE PORTER

Lilli Vanessi/Kate (Patricia Morison) and Fred Graham/Petruchio
(Alfred Drake) square off in a scene from *The Taming of the Shrew*,
from the original Broadway production of *Kiss Me, Kate* (Photofest).

ALWAYS TRUE TO YOU IN MY FASHION

Words and Music by
COLE PORTER

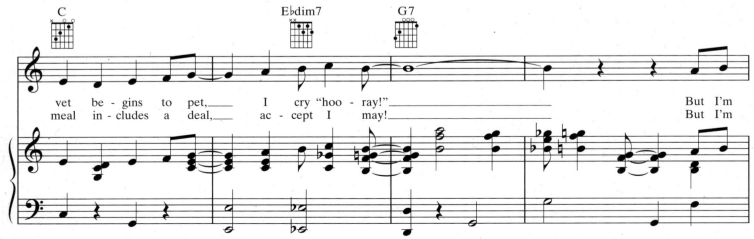

Always True to You in My Fashion - 4 - 1

Refrain 3:
There's a wealthy Hindu priest
Who's a wolf, to say the least,
When the priest goes too far east, I also stray.
But I'm always true to you, darlin', in my fashion,
Yes, I'm always true to you, darlin', in my way.
There's a lush from Portland, Ore.,
Who is rich but such a bore,
When the bore falls on the floor, I let him lay.
But I'm always true to you, darlin', in my fashion,
Yes, I'm always true to you, darlin', in my way.
Mister Harris, plutocrat,
Wants to give my cheek a pat,
If the Harris pat
Means a Paris hat,
Bébé, Oo-la-la!
Mais je suis toujours fidèle, darlin', in my fashion,
Oui, je suis toujours fidèle, darlin', in my way.

Refrain 4:
From Ohio, Mister Thorne
Calls me up from night 'til morn,
Mister Thorne once cornered corn and that ain't hay.
But I'm always true to you, darlin', in my fashion,
Yes, I'm always true to you, darlin', in my way.
From Milwaukee, Mister Fritz
Often moves me to the Ritz,
Mister Fritz is full of Schlitz and full of play.
But I'm always true to you, darlin', in my fashion,
Yes, I'm always true to you, darlin', in my way.
Mister Gable, I mean Clark,
Wants me on his boat to park,
If the Gable boat
Means a sable coat,
Anchors aweigh!
But I'm always true to you, darlin', in my fashion,
Yes, I'm always true to you, darlin', in my way.

BIANCA

**Words and Music by
COLE PORTER**

To win you, Bi - an - ca, there's noth - ing I would not do._____ I would glad - ly give up cof - fee for San - ka, e - ven San - ka, Bi - an - ca, for you!_____ 2. In the you!_____

BRUSH UP YOUR SHAKESPEARE

Bowery waltz tempo

Words and Music by
COLE PORTER

Vamp till ready

Verse:

girls to - day, in so - ci - e - ty, go for clas - si - cal

po - et - ry, so to win their hearts, one must quote with ease

start 'em sim - ply rav - in', _____ is the po - et peo - ple

call _____ "The bard of Strat-ford - on - A - von."

Refrain:
Play 3 times

1. Brush up your Shake - speare, start quot - ing him
2. Brush up your Shake - speare, start quot - ing him
3. Brush up your Shake - speare, start quot - ing him

Refrain 4:
Brush up your Shakespeare,
Start quoting him now.
Brush up your Shakespeare
And the women you will wow.
Better mention "The Merchant Of Venice"
When her sweet pound o' flesh you would menace.
If her virtue, at first, she defends – well,
Just remind her that "All's Well That Ends Well."
And if still she won't give you a bonus,
You know what Venus got from Adonis!
Brush up your Shakespeare
And they'll all kowtow.

Refrain 5:
Brush up your Shakespeare,
Start quoting him now.
Brush up your Shakespeare
And the women you will wow.
If your goil is a Washington Heights dream,
Treat the kid to "A Midsummer Night's Dream."
If she then wants an all-by-herself night,
Let her rest ev'ry 'leventh or "Twelfth Night."
If because of your heat she gets huffy,
Simply play on and "Lay on, Macduffy!"
Brush up your Shakespeare
And they'll all kowtow.

FROM THIS MOMENT ON

Words and Music by
COLE PORTER

the fu - ture looks so gay, now we are al - i - bied when we

Suddenly lively

say:_____

mf *accel. e cresc.*

℁ *Refrain: (lively but not rushed)*

From this mo - ment on,_____

mf

you for me, dear,

Interlude: (più mosso)

dear one, my fair one, my

sun - beam, my moon - beam, my

blue - bird, my love - bird, my

dream - boat, my cream puff, my

Molto agitato

I AM ASHAMED THAT WOMEN ARE SO SIMPLE

Words and Music by
COLE PORTER

I Am Ashamed That Women Are So Simple - 3 - 1

WE SHALL NEVER BE YOUNGER

Words and Music by
COLE PORTER

We Shall Never Be Younger - 4 - 1

WHAT DOES YOUR SERVANT DREAM ABOUT?

Words and Music by
COLE PORTER

Tempo I

Refrain:

won-der that your ser-vant has a cock-eyed point of view, for {he/she}

dreams all day of___ ev-'ry-thing gay, but {he/she} dreams the whole night through of

dirt, gar-bage, and you. Dirt, *slop,___* and you, *pew!*

That's what your ser-vant dreams a-bout the whole night through.